NIST Technical Note XXXX

LoopDA 3.0 - Natural Ventilation Design and Analysis Software User Guide

W. Stuart Dols
Steven J. Emmerich
Brian J. Polidoro

December 2011

U.S. Department of Commerce
John E. Bryson, Secretary
National Institute of Standards and Technology
Patrick D. Gallagher, Under Secretary of Commerce for Standards and Technology and Director

Abstract

LoopDA 3.0 is an update to version 1.0 of the natural ventilation design tool developed by the National Institute of Standards and Technology. This software tool can be utilized to determine the size of natural ventilation openings necessary to provide a airflow rates that satisfy design requirements based on minimum ventilation and cooling load requirements. The method employed is based largely upon the *Loop Equation Design Method* that provides for sizing of openings to utilize driving wind and stack pressures to achieve design airflow rates. This version implements a simple thermal design calculation to assist in determining design temperatures and airflow rates and provides a more streamlined interface to more efficiently implement the design process as compared to the previous version. A simple design example is also provided.

Key Words: airflow analysis; building energy; building technology; computer program; design tool; indoor air quality; multizone analysis; natural ventilation

Contents

Introduction

In earlier work [Dols and Emmerich 2003, Emmerich and Dols 2003], the National Institute of Standards and Technology (NIST) developed a software tool to implement the Loop Equation Design Method (presented in detail in [Emmerich et al. 2001]) which is a method for sizing of natural ventilation components that is general and practical and allows direct consideration of stack and wind-driven airflow that is critical in addressing natural ventilation airflow. The tool assists the designer in performing the needed steps of developing the natural ventilation system design including: establishing the global geometry and topology of zones and interconnecting flow paths, establishing design conditions, setting up and solving the representative loop equations based on the "design" form of the airflow components, and analyzing operation under a variety of conditions.

Version 1.0 of the LoopDA program (for **Loop D**esign and **A**nalysis tool), was developed as a version of CONTAM. LoopDA 1.0 has been upgraded to version 3.0 to correspond to the latest version of CONTAM 3.0. Further, LoopDA 3.0 has been modified to streamline the process of implementing the Loop Equation Design method mainly by eliminating the need for a third party spreadsheet during the design process and by assisting the estimate of design temperatures and airflow rates within the natural ventilation openings to be sized by incorporating a simple thermal design calculation. This document / help system provides an overview of the steps involved in implementing the Loop Equation Design within LoopDA 3.0, detailed input requirements, and a brief example of how to utilize the tool.

1

What's New

LoopDA 3.0 is an update to LoopDA 1.0. It is referred to as 3.0, because it utilizes the simulation engine of CONTAM 3.0 to perform the analysis. The following is a list of new features of version 3.0. Some of these features were influenced by the feedback provided by a design engineer who evaluated the usability of version 1.0 [Daly 2003].

Added a Simple Thermal Design Calculation

In version 1.0, the user was required to select a design airflow rate and temperature difference based on their judgment or external calculations. LoopDA 3.0 now provides a *simple thermal design* calculation that determines these values based on a new set of zone properties including: zone dimensions (floor area and external surface area), minimum airflow requirements, heat sources and overall heat transfer coefficient of the external surface area.

A Simple Thermal Design dialog box provides a list of available loops and associated zones along with relevant airflow requirements (minimum ventilation rate and cooling load). Users set the design airflow rate for each loop based on this information then execute the simple thermal design calculation to balance the airflow through the loops, set the design airflow rates for the natural ventilation airflow components (paths and ducts), then perform a steady-state heat transfer calculation to determine the resultant temperature of ventilation air for each of the airflow components.

Modified Loop Drawing

In LoopDA 1.0 the user was required to draw the complete pressure loop that started and ended at the same point on the SketchPad. Now one need only draw an "arrow" that indicates the intended paths the airflow is to take through the building. Begin drawing outside of the building through the desired flow paths and ducts and end just outside the path (or duct) through which the air is to exit. This provides a more conceptual view of how a designer might represent their intended airflow patterns.

Integrated Asymptotic Plots

LoopDA 1.0 required the user to export loop data to a text file, import the text file to a spreadsheet template, then utilize the spreadsheet to generate plots (asymptotic plots) of relationship between the sizes of the airflow paths and ducts associated with each loop. This was a cumbersome process to work with the different programs. The ability to generate and view these plots has been directly integrated into the program greatly streamlining the design process.

Streamlined LoopDA Interface

LoopDA 1.0 was largely based on the ContamW code base. This resulted in an interface that contained some unnecessary and somewhat cumbersome features. The following is a list of how the interface has been streamlined:

1. The menus have been reduced to include only LoopDA-related commands.

2. The icon placement menu only allows the drawing of LoopDA-related icons: zones, paths and annotations.

3. Wind pressure is now simply accounted for via a wind pressure coefficient provided for each individual envelope path or duct terminal.

4. Only those flow element types available in LoopDA are listed for selection (orifice, general powerlaw, self-regulating vent). The creation of each flow path or duct now automatically generates a distinct airflow or ductflow element.

5. Zone properties have been enhanced to support the simple thermal design calculation.

Simplified Analysis Calculation

The analysis calculation consists only of a steady airflow calculation by ContamX, so access to the simulation run control has been omitted. If one wishes to perform a more detailed calculation, the LoopDA project can be saved as a CONTAM project to utilize the full capability of CONTAM. A comparison between the design and analysis values is provided directly on the SketchPad.

Added a Self-regulating Vent

A self-regulating vent airflow component was added based on the work of James Axley [Axley 2001a].

The Loop Equation Design Method

The Loop Equation Design Method that is proposed for the Design Development stage of the overall design process of a natural ventilation system is described in detail in [Emmerich, et al. 2001]. (Note: The other design stages – Conceptual Design and Design Performance Evaluation – both precede and follow the Design Development Stage and are also described in [Emmerich, et al. 2001]. Detailed theory of the method is presented in [Axley 2001a] and [Axley 2001b].). The Loop Equation Design Method consists of the following eight steps:

1. Lay out the global geometry and multi-zone topology of the natural ventilation flow loops for each zone of the building.

2. Identify an ambient pressure node and additional pressure nodes at entries and exits of each flow component along the loops.

3. Establish design conditions: wind pressure coefficients for envelope flow components, ambient temperature, wind speed and direction, and interior temperatures; evaluate ambient and interior air densities.

4. Establish first-order design criteria (i.e., a ventilation objective) and apply continuity to determine the objective design airflow rates required for each natural ventilation flow component.

5. Form the forward loop equations for each loop established in step 1 above by systematically accounting for all pressure changes while traversing the loop.

6. Determine the minimum feasible sizes for each of the flow components by evaluating asymptotic limits of the loop equation for the design conditions.

7. Develop and apply a sufficient number of technical or non-technical design rules or constraints to transform the under-determined design problem defined by each loop equation into a determined problem.

8. Develop an appropriate operational strategy to accommodate the regulation of the natural ventilation system for variations in design conditions.

As detailed in the following section, the user will perform some of these steps explicitly (e.g., Step 1). Other steps are performed implicitly by LoopDA without user interaction (e.g., Step 5). Still others are accomplished by a combination of explicit and implicit actions (e.g., Step 3).

Using LoopDA

The LoopDA GUI consists of four main parts: menu, toolbar, SketchPad and status bar. These are provided to allow you to create and interact with a building representation that you can use to implement the Loop Equation Design Method.

NOTE: At any time while running the program, you can hit the F1 key to obtain context-sensitive help.

- **Menu** - The menu provides you with all the commands you will need to interact with LoopDA. Use the Alt key on the keyboard to display the hot keys associated with each command in the menu. This is a quick way to execute the menu commands. It is a good idea to explore the menu commands to become familiar with the features available in the program and to learn shortcuts associated with the commands.

- **Toolbar** - The toolbar simply provides access to a few of the most used items of LoopDA including the drawing tools. Hover over each button for a brief description of the tool.

- **SketchPad** - This is the large blank region of the program window in which you draw a schematic elevation view of a section of a building. This schematic basically consists of a set of icons on a grid of cells. You use the drawing tools and icon placement commands to draw the building walls and place building component icons, e.g., zones, airflow paths and ducts. You can use either the mouse or the arrow keys on the keyboard to maneuver around the SketchPad. Once the building is drawn, you view properties of the building components by highlighting icons on the SketchPad and hitting the enter key or simply double-clicking on the icon. Many icons will be red in color until you define their properties. Once defined, they will either become **black**, e.g., zones and airflow paths or **blue** for ducts.

- **Status Bar** - The status bar is located at the bottom of the window and provides you with information related to the currently highlighted cell on the SketchPad. This information can also be conveniently viewed in a tooltip window via the **View -> Options** menu command or pressing **Ctrl-T** on the keyboard.

Using the GUI to Implement the Loop Equation Design Method

The following step are those required to utilize LoopDA to implement the Loop Equation Design Method. Note that these steps do not align perfectly with those presented in the Loop Equation Design Method section, but they do address all of the steps needed to implement the method.

1. Define project default Design Data via the Calculations menu.

2. Use the Box and Line drawing tools provided in the toolbar to draw the outlines of the zones. This will form an elevation view of a section of the building through which natural ventilation is to be provided.

3. Right-click within the zones to place zone icons. Click on the icons and define the zone properties. Set the minimum required ventilation rates (e.g., based on ASHRAE Standard 62.1) and the thermal characteristics of the zone in order to establish the ventilative cooling airflow rate required to maintain the zone at a design temperature for the current design conditions.

4. Right click on the walls to place airflow path icons that connect the zones. You can also use the duct drawing tool to draw ducts. It is best to draw all the sections of a duct before defining them. A typical duct will have three sections: inlet fitting, segment, and outlet fitting, with each section separated by a junction icon. [See Drawing Ducts]

5. Define each of the flow paths and duct segments by double-clicking each undefined icon or segment in turn and setting the properties as desired via the associated dialog boxes that will be displayed. You will be prompted to select the type of airflow or duct flow element that is to represent the relationship between airflow and pressure drop through the flow path, e.g., powerlaw, orifice or self-regulating vent, or duct, e.g., segment or terminal/fitting.
    NOTE: You can verify the wind pressures on the paths and duct terminals adjacent to the ambient zone by switching to the *wind pressure mode* of the SketchPad via the View menu. This will display a scaled set of red lines that will indicate the relative pressure at each opening. The status bar/tool tip will provide the wind pressure at the currently selected envelope path or duct terminal icon.

6. Use the Loop (Arrow) drawing tool to draw intended airflow patterns (pressure loops) through the flow paths and ducts. Begin drawing outside of the building and draw in the direction that you want air to flow through the airflow paths. Drawing will stop when you have exited the building via a flow path or duct. Note that the arrows you draw represent the *pressure conservation* concept of the *Loop Equation Design Method*.

7. Define design conditions for the case you are working on via the Design Data dialog box available under the Calculations menu:

    o   outdoor temperature and wind speed

    o   zone cooling and heating set point temperatures: T_{csp} and T_{hsp}

8. Access the Simple Thermal Design dialog box via the Calculations menu to:

    a. review required airflow rates for each zone

    b. set airflow rates for each loop based on required airflow rates

    c. perform the Simple Thermal Design calculation to balance airflows and determine temperatures for each zone, airflow path and duct

9. Double click each loop arrow icon to reveal the Pressure Loop Properties dialog and review the asymptotic relationships between the components to be sized. This utilizes the inverse form of the airflow elements to present the feasible design curves. Set each component to be sized in turn until they have all been defined.

10. Steps 1 - 9 essentially form the design portion of the process for a given set of design conditions (e.g., outdoor temperature and wind speed). Once the design portion of the process has been completed for a given set of design conditions, use the Run Simulation command under the Calculation menu to perform an analysis calculation. This will calculate the airflow rates for the combination of sizes you selected.

11. After the simulation has been successfully run, the SketchPad will be set to the *results display mode*. In this mode, scaled lines will be displayed to provide relative airflow rates and pressure difference across each airflow path and duct terminal icon, and the status

bar/tool tip will provide numerical results. Airflow results will be provided in both mass flow and volume flow units along with the fractional bias between the mass flow as calculated by the simulation (Q_{sim}) and that determined via the Simple Thermal Design calculation (Q_{calc}).

$$FB = 2\frac{(Q_{sim} - Q_{calc})}{(Q_{sim} + Q_{calc})}$$

Fractional Bias (FB) provides a normalized range of values between ± 2.0 and is very similar to percent difference for values between ± 25 %. Values of FB between ± 1.636 indicate that averages are within one order of magnitude of each other, and values between ± 1.960 are within two orders of magnitude of each other.

12. Steps 7 through 11 are repeated for each set of design conditions thus establishing the range of sizes required to meet the various conditions that are expected to be encountered for the building. To perform these steps for another set of conditions you should save the project under a new name, <u>Unsize All Elements</u> via the Calculations menu, and repeat steps 7 through 11.

Design Data

Define the design weather conditions and provide default project values.

- **Weather**
  - o **Outdoor Temperature** - outdoor temperature for current design conditions.
  - o **Wind Speed** - wind speed for current design conditions
  - o **Atmospheric Pressure** - used to calculate air densities
- **Default Project Values**
  Provide default values to be used whenever you create a new zone in the project. These values can be overridden for specific zones as desired. See the Zone Properties dialog for detailed descriptions.

Zone Data

Zone data are used to establish ventilation requirements. Inputs are provided to establish minimum ventilation requirements that address building and occupant pollutant loads, for example, as provided by ASHRAE Standard 62.1. Inputs are also provided to address thermal loads to establish airflow rates for a given set of temperature conditions. You will use these properties to set airflow rates (for pressure loops) for specific design conditions when working with the Simple Thermal Design features of LoopDA.

Note that this set of properties is based on a very simplistic view of the zone in question, i.e., a cooling load calculation to determine Qcool that does not account for solar incidence on various building surfaces, fenestration effects, transient conduction, etc. (see Chapter 18 of [ASHRAE 2009]). However, you could use another load calculation tool to obtain the zone cooling load and simply utilize the inputs provided herein to accommodate those values, e.g., determine the total cooling load with another tool and simply enter the value as the Other Heat Gain parameter.

- **Zone Name** - Each zone name must be unique.
- **Dimensions**
  - **Volume** (V_z) - used to determine the zone air change rate.
  - **Floor Area** (A_f) - multiplied by the *Ventilation per Floor Area* to determine the minimum ventilation rate.
  - **Envelope Surface Area** (A_s) - used to determine the *Required Airflow* of the *Thermal Design Parameters* to account for thermal conductivity through the building envelope.
- **Minimum Ventilation Requirements**
  - **Ventilation per Person** (R_p) - ventilation rate requirement due to occupant-generated pollutant load
  - **Occupant Density** (D_{occ}) - number of persons per floor area
  - **# of Persons** (N_p)- total number of occupants = $D_{occ}A_f$
  - **Ventilation per Floor Area** (R_a) - required ventilation based on building pollutant load
  - **Minimum Ventilation Rate** (Q_{min}) - minimum ventilation requirement = $R_pN_p + R_aA_f$
- **Thermal Design Parameters** - are used to determine the cooling load to be overcome via natural ventilative cooling. These values will be used by the Simple Thermal Design calculation to calculate the design temperatures and airflow rates for the natural ventilation openings.
  - **Design Temperature** (T_{des}) - desired temperature for current design conditions. If this is an unoccupied zone, e.g., a vent shaft, then this temperature may not be too relevant to your design. It will be determined by the simple thermal design calculation.
  - **Heat Transfer Coefficient** (U) - for conduction through the building envelope surface (enter a value of 0.0 to ignore conduction)

- o **Internal Heat Gain** (q_{int}) - heat sources having a per floor area basis

- o **Other Heat Gain** (q_{oth}) - other heat sources specific to this zone

- o **Int + Other Heat Gain** (q_{total}) - summation of internal and other heat sources = $q_{int}A_f + q_{oth}$

- o **Conductive Heat Gain** (q_{cond}) - cooling load due to conductive heat transfer through the Envelope Surface Area = $U A_s (T_{out} - T_{des})$

- o **Required Airflow** (Q_{cool}) - is the outdoor airflow at temperature T_{ambt} that would be required to maintain the zone at the design temperature provided above. This flow rate is provided in the units set for the Minimum Ventilation Rate and as an air changes rate (1/h).

$$Q_{cool} = \frac{UA_s(T_{ambt} - T_{des}) + \dot{q}_{int}A_f + \dot{q}_{other}}{\rho C_p (T_{des} - T_{ambt})}$$

- **Temperature Set Points** The outdoor temperature is used to determine the cooling load. The set point and balance point temperatures are provided here as a reference when setting the design temperature and for comparison to T_{calc} once the Simple Thermal Design calculation has been performed.

  - o **Outdoor** (T_{ambt}) - outdoor (ambient) temperature for current design conditions. Click the Edit... button to define design data and set this value.

  - o **Heating Set Point** (T_{hsp}) - thermostat set point during heating season, e.g., winter.

  - o **Cooling Set Point** (T_{csp}) - thermostat set point during cooling season, e.g., summer

  - o **Heating Balance Point** (T_{hbp}) - outdoor temperature at which the combined ventilative and conductive heat loss from the zone just offsets the internal gains (based on a steady state approximation and a minimum ventilation rate). Below this temperature, the air is too cold to balance the heat generated within the zone and maintain T_{hsp}.

$$T_{hbp} = T_{hsp} - \frac{q_{total}}{\rho Q_{min} C_p + \sum UA_s}$$

- **Loop-calculated Values**
  These values are determined by the Simple Thermal Design calculation. They are provided here for comparison with the design values entered into this dialog.

  - o **Temperature** (T_{calc}) - is the temperature that will result in this zone once the simple thermal design calculation has been performed.

  - o **Airflow Rate** (Q_{calc}) - is the volume flow of air out of this zone based on the density of air within the zone. This value is based on the loop flows through the zone.

Path Types

Select the type of path you wish to create. These are mathematical models that relate the airflow to the pressure difference across the path. These are akin to the airflow elements in CONTAM, but LoopDA provides both forward and inverse forms of the model. The inverse forms of the equations are used when forming the pressure loop equations during the sizing phase of the design procedure, while the forward forms are used when performing a simulation to verify the design.

LoopDA currently supports the following types:

- **General Powerlaw** - the general form of the relationship between airflow rate and pressure drop across an opening.

  o Forward form: $Q = C \, \Delta P^n$

  o Inverse form: $\Delta P = \left(\dfrac{Q}{C} \right)^{\frac{1}{n}}$

- **Orifice** - the form of the powerlaw relationship that provides for input in terms of the cross sectional area and the flow coefficient of an orifice.

  o Forward form: $Q = C_d A \sqrt{2/\rho} \, \Delta P^n$

  o Inverse form: $\Delta P = \left(\dfrac{Q\sqrt{\rho/2}}{C_d A} \right)^{\frac{1}{n}}$

- **Self-regulating Vent** - limits the airflow rate in both directions through a flow path with user-defined limiting air pressure differences. LoopDA implements the self-regulating vent as described in Axley 2001.

  o Forward form:

  positive pressure drop $\quad Q^+ = Q_0 \left(1.0 - e^{\frac{-\Delta P}{\Delta P_0}} \right)$

  negative pressure drop $\quad Q^- = -f Q_0 \left(1.0 - e^{\frac{\Delta P}{f \Delta P_0}} \right)$

  o Inverse form: $\quad \Delta P = -\Delta P_0 \, ln\left(1.0 - \dfrac{Q}{Q_0} \right)$

Airflow Path Properties

There are two dialog box tabs of data associated with each airflow path. The Flow Path tab is common to all flow paths, and the other tab provides data specific to the type of inverse airflow element you select to associate with the given path.

- **Path Number** - an automatically generated number. Numbers are assigned as you create the paths and renumbered whenever you save the file. Paths are renumbered so that they increase from left-to-right and top-to-bottom on the SketchPad.

- **Elevation** - the height of the center of the opening from ground level. It is only used to calculate the stack pressure.

- **Wind Pressure Coefficient** (C_p) - provides the directional and/or building geometry dependent component of wind pressure as in the following equation.

$$\Delta P_{wind} = \frac{1}{2} \rho C_p u_{wind}^2$$

ρ = density of air [kg/m^3]

u = wind speed [m/s]

NOTE: This implementation does not account for the wind speed modifier separately as can be done with CONTAM. You must account for the wind speed modifier via the wind pressure coefficient. For a more detailed treatment refer to Working with Weather and Wind in the CONTAM Manual [Walton and Dols 2005] and Chapter 24 of [ASHRAE 2009].

- **Loop-calculated Values**
  These values are determined by the simple thermal design calculation.

  o **Temperature (Tcalc)** - the temperature of the air that flows into this path once the simple thermal design calculation has been performed.

  o **Airflow Rate (Qcalc)** - the volume flow of air into this path based on the density of air upstream. This value is based on the loop flows through the path as set via the simple thermal design dialog.

Powerlaw Properties

These are the properties of the general powerlaw airflow element type.

- **Element Name** - a unique identifier you assign to the powerlaw airflow element that is associated with this airflow path. If you choose to work with this airflow element in ContamW, you can export as a CONTAM project, and this element will become available for general use as is the case for all airflow elements in ContamW.

- **CDP Data** - Characteristic Design Parameter information for this specific airflow path.

  o **CDP Name** - an automatically generated name assigned to this path. It will be used to identify the path when plotting asymptotes during the sizing procedure of the loop equation design process. The path number will be appended to this name to uniquely identify it.

- Flow Coefficient (C) - The coefficients may only be expressed in SI units due to the conversion method used. Use the following conversion to convert from IP units to SI units:

  To convert from IP units of $\frac{cfm}{(in.H_2O)^n}$ to SI units of $\frac{m^3/s}{Pa^n}$ multiply by $\frac{1}{2119 \times 249^n}$

- Sized / Unsized - set to "sized" once you have determined the final value of the CDP for the current set of design conditions. This value will then be used to determine the contribution of this path to the total pressure drop as loops are traversed to form the pressure loop equations. In essence, once sized these values are moved to the right hand side of the pressure loop equation.

- **Flow Exponent** (n) - varies from 0.5 for large openings where the flow is dominated by dynamic effects, and 1.0 for narrow openings dominated by viscous effects. Measurements usually indicate a flow exponent of 0.6 to 0.7 for typical infiltration openings (see section 5.2 of [CIBSE 1997]).

- **Description** - You can provide a more detailed note to describe this airflow element.

- **Icon** - Choose either the small or large opening icon as appropriate for the specific airflow element. The icon has no effect on the calculations.

Orifice Properties

These are the properties of the orifice airflow element type.

- **Element Name** - is the unique identifier you assign to the orifice airflow element that is associated with this airflow path. If you choose to work with this airflow element in ContamW, you can export as a CONTAM project, and this element will become available for general use as is the case for all airflow elements in ContamW.

- **CDP Data** - Characteristic Design Parameter information for this specific airflow path.

  - **CDP Name** - is an automatically generated name assigned to this path. It will be used to identify the path when plotting asymptotes during the sizing procedure of the loop equation design process. The path number will be appended to this name to uniquely identify it.

  - **Orifice Area** - is the cross-sectional area of the orifice

  - **Sized / Unsized** - set to "sized" once you have determined the final value of the CDP for the current set of design conditions. This value will then be used to determine the contribution of this path to the total pressure drop as loops are traversed to form the pressure loop equations. In essence, once sized these values are moved to the right hand side of the pressure loop equation.

- **Flow Exponent** (n) - varies from 0.5 for large openings where the flow is dominated by dynamic effects, and 1.0 for narrow openings dominated by viscous effects. Measurements usually indicate a flow exponent of 0.6 to 0.7 for typical infiltration openings.

- **Discharge Coefficient** (C_d) - is related to the dynamic effects and is typically close to 0.6 for a sharp-edged orifice and slightly higher for other openings in buildings (see section 5.3 of [CIBSE 1997] and chapter 16 of [ASHRAE 2009]).

- **Hydraulic Diameter** (D_h) - The hydraulic diameter is equal to (4 × Area / Perimeter). For square openings this equals the square root of the area, and for long thin openings it is two times the width.

- **Reynolds Number** - The transition from laminar flow to turbulent flow occurs over a broad range of Reynolds numbers with the flow being fully laminar approximately below 100.

  Note: The hydraulic diameter and Reynolds number have little impact on the calculations. Generally you should use the default values except for special circumstances where you need them to be modified. The parameters above describe the flow characteristics of an orifice in typical operation. At extremely low pressure drops the use of the powerlaw model leads to a division by zero during the network solution process. This problem is avoided during simulations by changing to a linear model in this region. The model is based conceptually on the flow changing from turbulent to laminar at very low pressures. The Hydraulic diameter and Reynolds number are used to determine a point where the model changes from the powerlaw to linear.

- **Description** - You can provide a more detailed note to describe this airflow element.

- **Icon** - Choose either the small or large opening icon as appropriate for the specific airflow element. The icon has no effect on the calculations.

Self-regulating Vent Properties

These are the properties of the self-regulating vent airflow element type.

- **Element Name** - a unique identifier you assign to the self-regulating vent airflow element that is associated with this airflow path. If you choose to work with this airflow element in ContamW, you can export as a CONTAM project, and this element will become available for general use as is the case for all airflow elements in ContamW.

- **CDP Data** - Characteristic Design Parameter information for this specific airflow path.

  o **CDP Name** - an automatically generated name assigned to this path. It will be used to identify the path when plotting asymptotes during the sizing procedure of the loop equation design process. The path number will be appended to this name to uniquely identify it.

  o **Maximum Flow Rate** (Q_0) - an empirical value that sets the maximum airflow rate that this element will allow to pass through an airflow path.

  o **Sized / Unsized** - set to "sized" once you have determined the final value of the CDP for the current set of design conditions. This value will then be used to determine the contribution of this path to the total pressure drop as loops are traversed to form the pressure loop equations. In essence, once sized these values are moved to the right hand side of the pressure loop equation.

- **Regulating Pressure** (ΔP_0) - an empirical value that represents the approximate pressure difference above which the airflow will be limited to the maximum flow rate Q_0.

- **Reverse Flow Fraction** (f) - the fraction of the Maximum Flow Rate to which the airflow through this element will be limited when the pressure difference is negative across the airflow path.

- **Description** - You can provide a more detailed note to describe this airflow element.

- **Icon** - Choose either the small or large opening icon as appropriate for the specific airflow element. The icon has no effect on the calculations.

Drawing Ducts

You draw ducts in LoopDA exactly as done in ContamW. However, in LoopDA, you are working in the elevation view. [See Working with Ducts in the CONTAM User Guide]. You should draw duct segments for each inlet, airflow segment and outlet of a duct as shown in the figure below. This will provide a separate term in the loop equation for each component of the duct system. When referring to the SketchPad, the icons that make up the duct are referred to as *Terminal*, *Segment* and *Junction icons* as shown in the figure below. When referring to the sizing components, you will work with the segment icons to associate a duct element type of either *Terminal/Fitting* or *Segment* as shown in the figure. This will become more apparent as you work with the program.

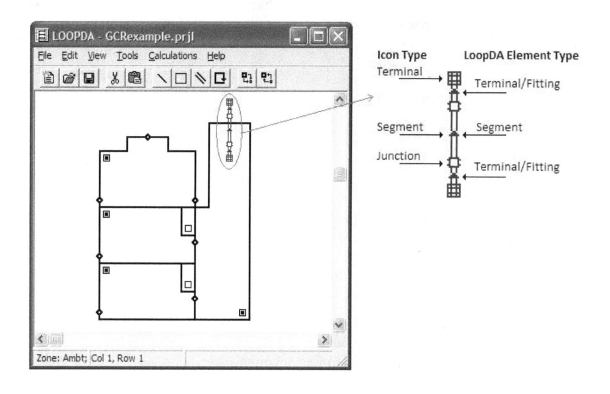

15

Duct Type

Select the type of duct you wish to create. These are mathematical models that relate the airflow to the pressure difference through a duct. These are akin to the duct flow elements in CONTAM, but LoopDA provides both forward and inverse forms of the model. The inverse forms of the equations are used when forming the pressure loop equations during the sizing phase of the design procedure, while the forward forms are used when performing a simulation to verify the design.

LoopDA implements the Darcy-Colebrook duct flow element of CONTAM in two forms: one accounting for the friction losses along the length of a duct *segment* and another accounting for dynamic losses at a *terminal/fitting*. The general forward form of the Darcy-Colebrook element is as follows:

$$Q = \sqrt{\frac{2A^2 \Delta P}{\rho (fL/D_h + \sum C_l)}}$$

- The inverse form for the *segment* type (friction loss):

$$\Delta P = \frac{\rho Q^2}{2A^2} \frac{fL}{D_h} = \frac{8\rho f L Q^2}{\pi^2 D_h^5}$$

  Note that C_l does not appear in the segment equation.

- The inverse form for the *terminal/fitting* type (dynamic or local loss):

$$\Delta P = \frac{\rho Q^2}{2A^2} \sum C_l$$

  Note that L does not appear in the terminal/fitting equation.

Duct Properties

There are two tabs of data associated with each duct segment icon. The Duct tab is common to all duct segment icons, and the other tab provides data specific to whether the duct is being used to represent a *segment* or a *terminal/fitting*. Segments have a length component associated with them that accounts for friction losses, and terminal/fittings have a loss coefficient associated with them that accounts for dynamic losses. The Duct page will enable or disable these items, Length and Sum of Loss Coefficient, depending on the type of duct you created. In either case the Darcy-Colebrook model is being used as outlined in the CONTAM documentation.

- **Duct Number** - an automatically generated number. Numbers are assigned as you create the ducts and renumbered whenever you save the file. Ducts are renumbered so that they increase from left-to-right and top-to-bottom on the SketchPad.
- **Length** - the length of the duct segment. This will only be enabled if you've set the type to be a segment and disabled if you selected terminal/fitting.

- **Sum of Loss Coefficients** - the local loss coefficient attributed to dynamic losses in the duct terminal/fitting. This will only be enabled if you've set the type to be a terminal/fitting and disabled if you selected segment.

- **Heat Gain** - used to provide a heat source at this duct in much the same way as can be done with a zone. This will only be enabled if you've set the type to be a segment and disabled if you selected terminal/fitting.

- **Loop-calculated Values**
  These values are determined by the simple thermal design calculation.

  o **Temperature (Tcalc)** - the temperature of the air that flows into this duct.

  o **Airflow Rate (Qcalc)** - the volume flow of air into this duct based on the density of air upstream. This value is based on the loop flows through the path as set via the simple thermal design dialog.

Duct Segment

Properties of a *segment* type duct element. This is implementing the friction loss component of the Darcy-Weisbbach equation presented in Chapter 21 of [ASHRAE 2009].

- **Element Name** - a unique identifier you assign to the duct component that is associated with this duct segment icon. If you choose to work with this duct in ContamW, you can export as a CONTAM project, and this will become available for general use as is the case for all duct elements in ContamW.

- **CDP Data** - Characteristic Design Parameter information for this specific duct.

  o **CDP Name** - an automatically generated name assigned to this duct. It will be used to identify the duct when plotting asymptotes during the sizing procedure of the loop equation design process. The duct number will be appended to this name to uniquely identify it.

  o **Diameter** - the effective diameter of the cross-sectional area of the duct.

  o **Sized / Unsized** - set to "sized" once you have determined the final value of the CDP for the current set of design conditions. This value will then be used to determine the contribution of this duct segment to the total pressure drop as loops are traversed to form the pressure loop equations. In essence, once sized, these values are moved to the right hand side of the pressure loop equation.

- **Friction Factor** - is dependant on the roughness of the duct wall and Reynolds number. Therefore, it is indeterminable until the airflow rate, and hence the velocity in the duct, are known. As provided below, you can estimate a design friction factor.

- **Description** - You can provide a more detailed note to describe this duct flow element.

- **Estimate Friction Factor** - Use the following to estimate the friction factor to be used during the sizing stage of the design process. The friction factor is calculated based on the Colebrook equation also presented in Chapter 21 of [ASHRAE 2009]. Once the sizing has been completed you can run the simulation to determine how significant the difference is between the design and analysis results and adjust the design values of this segment until the analysis flow matches the design flow to your level of satisfaction.

- o **Roughness** - of the duct wall
- o **Velocity** - Estimated velocity through the duct. You can revisit this once you have "sized" this duct and obtained the loop-calculated airflow (Q_{calc}).
- o **Hydraulic Diameter** (D_h) - is either an estimated value or the value once the duct has been sized.
- o **Reynolds Number** (Re) - calculated based on the above estimated values, the standard density of air (1.2041 kg/m^3) and dynamic viscosity (1.81625 x 10^{-5} N-s/m^2).

$$Re = \frac{\rho D_h V}{\mu}$$

Duct Terminal/Fitting

Properties of a *terminal/fitting* type duct element. This is implementing the dynamic or local loss component of the Darcy-Weisbbach equation presented in Chapter 21 of [ASHRAE 2009].

- **Element Name** - is the unique identifier you assign to the duct element that is associated with this duct segment icon. If you choose to work with this duct element in ContamW, you can export as a CONTAM project, and this element will become available for general use as is the case for all duct elements in ContamW.

- **CDP Data** - Characteristic Design Parameter information for this specific duct.
  - o **CDP Name** - an automatically generated name assigned to this duct. It will be used to identify the duct when plotting asymptotes during the sizing procedure of the loop equation design process. The duct number will be appended to this name to uniquely identify it.
  - o **Area** - the cross-sectional area of the duct.
  - o **Sized / Unsized** - set to "sized" once you have determined the final value of the CDP for the current set of design conditions. This value will then be used to determine the contribution of this duct terminal/fitting to the total pressure drop as loops are traversed to form the pressure loop equations. In essence, once sized, these values are moved to the right hand side of the pressure loop equation.

- **Description** - You can provide a more detailed note to describe this duct flow element.

Duct Junction

Duct junctions form the ends of duct runs and connections between duct segments and terminals/fittings. In LoopDA, they are akin to zones in that they will have a design temperature associated with them (T_{calc} below). They are also akin to paths in that they are the means to establish elevations of the ends of duct segments and to apply wind pressure effects when they are located in the ambient zone.

- **Junction Number** - is an automatically generated number. Numbers are assigned as you create the paths and renumbered whenever you save the file. Paths are renumbered so that they increase from left-to-right and top-to-bottom on the SketchPad.

- **Elevation** - the height of the duct junction from ground level. It is used to calculate the stack pressure for design and analysis purposes.

- **Wind Pressure Coefficient** (C_p) - provides the directional and/or building geometry dependent component of wind pressure as in the following equation. This will only be enabled if the junction is in the ambient zone.

$$\Delta P_{wind} = \frac{1}{2} \rho C_p u_{wind}^2$$

- **Loop-calculated Values**
  These values are determined by the simple thermal design calculation.

  o **Temperature (Tcalc)** - the temperature of the air that flow into this junction once the simple thermal design calculation has been performed.

  o **Airflow Rate (Qcalc)** - the volume flow of air into this junction based on the density of air upstream. This value is based on the loop flows through the junction as set via the simple thermal design dialog.

Simple Thermal Design

The main purpose of the Simple Thermal Design calculation is to determine the temperatures of the air flowing through the natural ventilation airflow components (paths and ducts) to be sized[1]. This provides the stack pressures that will be available to drive natural ventilation airflow rates. Use the Simple Thermal Design dialog to review required airflow rates, set loop airflow rates, and calculate the resultant zone and airflow component temperatures.

There are essentially two sets of calculation performed: one is a mass balance of flows to determine the resultant flows through the natural ventilation airflow components that have more than one loop passing through them[2], and the other is a steady-state energy balance to determine the temperatures that result in these zones given the outdoor air temperature, heat inputs of each zone and airflow rates through the zones.

The steady state energy balance equation is provided below.

$$\sum_{inlets} \dot{m}_j C_p T_j - \sum_{outlets} \dot{m}_i C_p T_i + U A_s (T_{ambt} - T_i) + \sum_{\substack{heat \\ sources}} \dot{q}_i = 0$$

The first two terms are convective heat gain/loss via airflow into/out of the zone, the next term is the conductive heat loss through the envelope surface area based on an overall heat transfer coefficient and the final term is the sum of heat sources (internal, solar, etc.). Note that this is a very simplistic cooling load calculation to determine Qcool that does not account for solar incidence on various building surfaces, fenestration effects, transient conduction, etc. (see Chapter 18 of [ASHRAE 2009]).

- **Loop Airflow Rates** - Use these controls to set the airflow rates for each loop in the project.
    - **Loop #** and **Design Airflow** - Select the loop for which you want to set a flow from this list. This will also change the set of components displayed in the Loop Component Data section of this dialog.
    - **Set Airflow Rate** - Set the desire units and flow rate then click the "**<< Update**" button to set the airflow rate of the currently selected loop. Be careful to apportion the flow rates to the loops when a single inlet provides airflow for multiple outlets. When an outlet serves multiple inlets, the airflow balance will properly determine the total flow through the outlet.
- **Perform Simple Thermal Design Calculation** - Once you have set all of the loop airflow rates, click this button. This will perform the mass and energy balance calculations to determine Tcalc and Qcalc for all of the Zones, Paths and Ducts associated with the loops.
- **Loop Component Data** - provides a list of building components (zones, paths and ducts) through which the currently selected loop passes. The components are presented in the order in which the air is intended to flow through them.
    - **Type** - is the type of component: Zone, Path or Duct
    - **Name** - provides the name of the component (zone or element name)

- o **#** - is the number of the component as provided when it is highlighted on the SketchPad
- o **Tcsp** - the cooling set point temperature for zones is provided for comparison to Tcalc
- o **Thsp** - the heating set point temperature for zones is provided for comparison to Tcalc
- o **Tcalc** - the temperature determined by the simple thermal design calculation. If the zone receives air directly from the ambient, then Tcalc should be the same as the design temperature that you set for the zone. This may not be the case if the zone receives air from one or more other zones that have heat sources associated with them.
- o **Qmin** - the minimum ventilation airflow rate for the zones. Use this value to help you decide the Design Airflow rate for the loop which would typically be the greater of this or Qcool. If Qmin is greater than Qcool then the zone is likely to be "over-cooled" and require supplemental heat.
- o **Qcool** - the ventilation airflow rate required to maintain the design temperature of a zone. Use this value to help you decide the Design Airflow rate for the loop. If Qcool is greater than Qmin then setting the loop airflow rate to Qcool would satisfy the minimum ventilation requirement as well.
- o **Qcalc** - the volumetric airflow rate determined by the simple thermal design calculation. This will either be the same as the mass flow rate of the associated loop or determined by the mass balance if more than one loop flows through the component. You can convert these values to mass flows at standard density as follows:

$Q_{std} = Qcalc \ \rho_{air}/\rho_{std} = Qcalc \ T_{std}/T$
where $T_{std} = 293.15$ and $T = Tcalc + 273.15$ (assuming Tcalc is provided in degrees Celsius).

---

1. This new feature provides the temperatures based on a steady-state energy balance, whereas LoopDA version 1.0 required the user to "guess" at these temperatures.

2. This new feature provides the necessary mass balance constraint that LoopDA version 1.0 did not.

Pressure Loop Properties

This dialog box provides the properties of a selected loop. Its main use is to provide you with minimum sizes of the flow components to be sized and to provide plots[1] of asymptotic relationships between the characteristic design parameters (CDP) of the loop components.

- **Loop Number** - is the number of the loops for which properties are being displayed.

- **Driving Pressures** - provides the **wind** and **stack pressures** and associated **wind speed** and **outdoor temperature** being used to determine the properties displayed in the *Component* section below. These are essentially the values used to determine the right hand side (RHS) of the Loop Equation provided here in general form:

$$\sum_{unsized} \Delta P_i = \Delta P_{stack} + \Delta P_{wind} - \sum_{sized} \Delta P_j$$

where:

ΔP_i = those loop flow elements that have not yet been sized

ΔP_{stack} = the driving pressure due to stack effect

ΔP_{wind} = the driving pressure due to wind

ΔP_j = those loop flow elements that have been sized are moved to the right-hand side of the loop equation.

- **Total Pressure Drop (RHS)** - provides the summation of the driving pressures (positive) and the sized components (negative) as shown in the equation above. The idea is to determine the size of the components that will provide a total pressure drop through them that is equal to that of the driving pressures for which you are designing, e.g., **wind & stack** or **stack only**. Once this has been accomplished, the corresponding RHS should be close to zero. This will become negative if the pressure drop through the sized components exceeds that of the driving pressures.

- **Natural Ventilation Airflow Component Size Data** - is a list of the loop components (paths and ducts) through which the loop passes. Highlight the element in the list that you would like to have other element pressure drops plotted against in the asymptotic plot.

  - **Type** - indicates if the item is either a path or duct

  - **#** - indicates the component number assigned by the SketchPad numbering scheme

  - **Name** - of the CDP with the component number appended. These names will be used when plotting the size relationships (asymptote plots). The type dependent prefixes are as follows:

Orifice	Aorfc (cross sectional orifice area)
General powerlaw	Ce (flow coefficient)
Self-regulating vent (Axley model)	Q0 (flow limit)
Duct segment (length)	D (equivalent diameter)
Duct terminal/fitting (sum of local loss coefficients)	A (effective area of terminal/fitting)

  - **Minimum Opening Size** - If the opening has not yet been sized, then this provides the minimum based on the current total pressure drop that remains. Note that these minima will change as more components are sized and moved to the RHS. So, they only apply to those items that are currently not sized.

- **Stack & Wind** - is the minimum value (asymptote) of the CDP that would provide the current total pressure drop (equal to the RHS of the loop equation) including both stack and wind pressure terms

- **Stack Only** - is the minimum value (asymptote) of the CDP that would provide the current total pressure drop equivalent to the RHS of the loop equation including only the stack pressure term.

o **Sized** - indicates whether or not you've set the size of the item via the associated properties. Once all the items of all the loops have been sized, then you can run the analysis calculation or simulation.

o **Value** - is the current value of the CDP. Even if a value is displayed here, the component only contributes to the Total Pressure Drop (RHS) if the Sized property is "yes".

o **dP** - is the pressure drop associated with those components that have been sized.

- **Size Relationship Graphs** - Select the curves to display on the plot (asymptote plots). This allows you to compare the relationships for the stack & wind and stack only curves.

- **Export Loop Data** - This feature is provided for compatibility with the previous version of LoopDA[1]. A spreadsheet template file is provided with the program into which the exported text file can be pasted. You can provide an optional **Name** and **Description** that will appear at the top of the file that you export. Click the **Export...** button to display a Save As... dialog box.

---

1. Version 1.0 of LoopDA did not provide asymptotic plots. It provided a means to export the data presented here. This capability is still retained to provide the user with the ability to explore this data in more detail outside of the LoopDA program. This allows you to evaluate the details of the loop equation parameters and manipulate the data and plots for advanced evaluation techniques, e.g., constraining duct segment and terminals sizes to be the same [Axley 2001a].

Calculations Menu

This menu provides access to various features related to the design and analysis calculations of LoopDA. Details of the Design Data and Simple Thermal Design items are provided in similarly titled sections of this document.

- **Design Data** - Open the project <u>Design Data</u> dialog box.

- **Simple Thermal Design** - Open the <u>Simple Thermal Design</u> dialog.

- **Run Simulation** - Perform the analysis calculation using the current design values. This utilizes the ContamX calculation engine to perform a steady state airflow calculation. Use this to verify that the analysis values (airflow rates) are close to those of the design values for each flow path. View the results for each flow path by revealing the icon tooltip and checking the Fractional Bias (FB) value between Qsim and Qcalc. (see <u>Using LoopDA</u>)

- **Unsize All Elements** - Select this to set all the sized airflow paths and ducts to be "Unsized". You would do this in order to perform the sizing design process for another set of design conditions using the same building configuration. For example, you have sized the natural ventilation airflow components for the Stack & Wind conditions and you now want to size them for the Stack only conditions.

- **Export CONTAM Project** - save LoopDA project file (.PRJL) as a CONTAM project file (.PRJ). This allows you to utilize the full set of features available in CONTAM to perform more detailed analysis on this project including: developing full geometry of the building, utilizing airflow elements you created in this project, performing contaminant analysis, etc.

  Note that upon opening the exported PRJ file with ContamW, it will still be an elevation view of the building. You can still perform analysis on this building section with CONTAM, but you will need to modify the building representation significantly to implement a plan view of the building as is normally done with CONTAM. The exporting feature allows you to have easy access to the airflow models that you defined via the design method in LoopDA.

Design Example - Classroom

The following provides a brief tutorial on how to utilize LoopDA to size the natural ventilation openings for a single zone case. The figure below provides a schematic diagram of a cross section of the room. This example is based on a case provided by [Daly 2003].

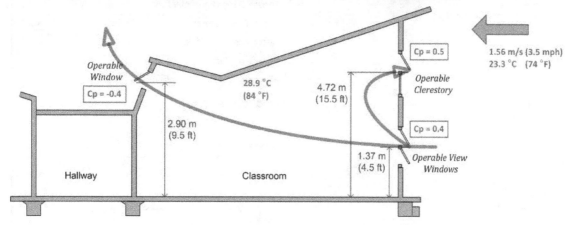

Conceptualization of Classroom Natural Ventilation Design

Run LoopDA and edit the Design Data to set the following:

- Outdoor Temperature = 23.3 °C (74 °F)

- Wind Speed = 1.56 m/s (3.5 mph)

- Indoor Design Temperature = 28.9 °C (84 °F)

- Room dimensions: 12.19 m x 7.32 m x 3.96 m (L x W x H_{avg}) (40 ft x 24 ft x 13 ft)

Draw the SketchPad diagram as shown below. Begin by drawing the zone outline, place the zone icon, and then each of the path icons.

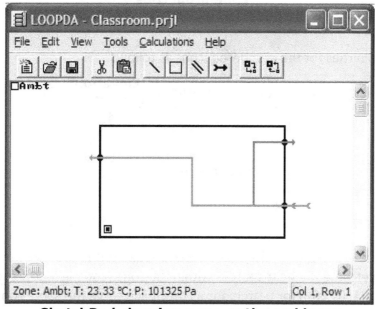

SketchPad showing zone, paths and loops

Define the zone and path icons as provided in the dialog box figures that follow.

Zone properties

Define the path properties for the numbered icons as follows:

Number	Type	Name	Elevation m (ft)	Cp
1	Orifice	Clerestory	4.72 (15.5)	0.5
2	Orifice	UpperWindow	2.90 (9.5)	-0.4
3	Orifice	InletWindow	1.37 (4.5)	0.4

Open the Simple Thermal Design dialog box via the Calculations menu. Set the airflow rates for the two loops to overcome the heat sources within the zone (cooling load). The value of Qcool should be 188.8 L/s (4000 cfm) for both loops as they each serve the same zone. Because both loops enter through the same flow path, you need to apportion some of the flow to each loop.

26

Set the design flow of each loop to 944 L/s (2000 cfm) and click the Perform Simple Thermal Design Calculation button. The results for both loops should appear as shown in the figure below. Note that the loop components are provided from top to bottom in the order in which the air flows through them: 1888 L/s (4000 cfm) of flow into path 3 (InletWindow) and then 961.7 L/s (2038 cfm) flow out of both paths 1 and 2. Note that in order for a mass balance to be maintained, a greater volume of 28.89 °C (84 °F) air must flow out due to the lower density of the exiting air.

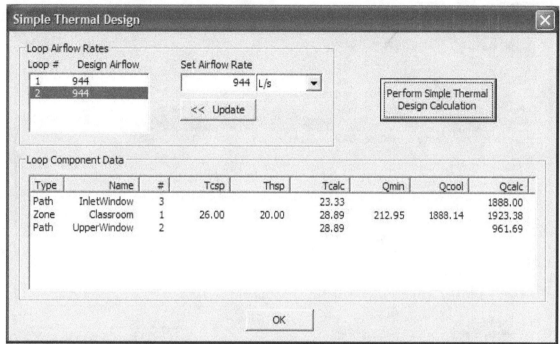

Simple Thermal Design Dialog box showing the result of Loop 1 after calculation has been performed

Now that the simple thermal design has been performed, the airflow rates and temperatures for each of the airflow paths (and zone) will be set. When you open each of the corresponding dialog boxes, this will be evident by the Qcalc and Tcalc values presented therein. It is now time to set the sizes of each airflow component.

Starting by double clicking Loop 2 (through paths 3 and 1) to reveal the Pressure Loop Properties dialog box shown below.

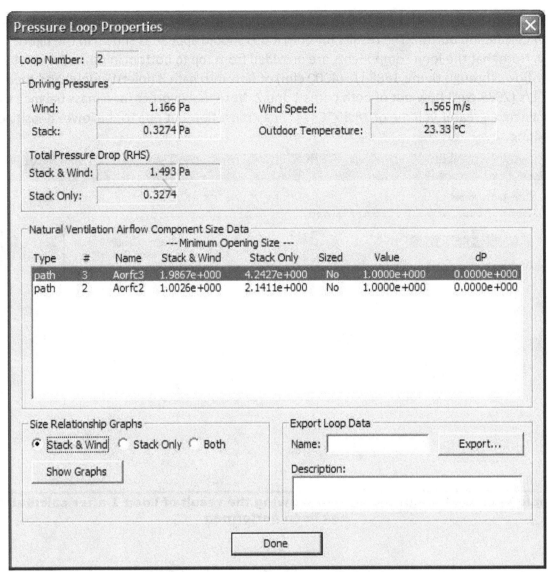

Pressure Loop Properties dialog box

Click the "Show Graphs" button to reveal the size relationship graph between the two openings (Aorfc3 and Aorfc2) shown below.

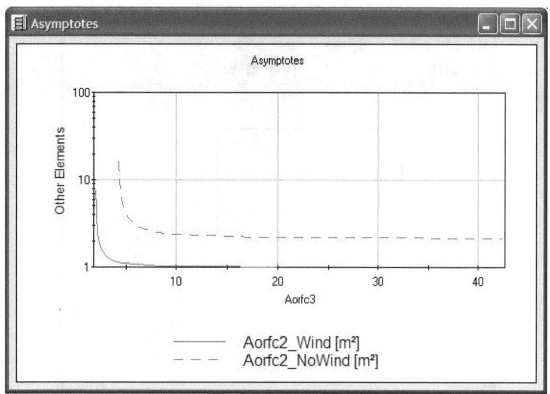

Plot showing relationship between sizes of two openings for both the Wind & Stack and Wind only design conditions

The dialog box indicates the minimum value for Aorfc3 is approximately 2 m^2 (21.53 ft^2) for the Stack & Wind condition and 4.2 m^2 (45.21 ft^2) for the Stack Only condition. The chart reveals that a value of 10 m^2 (107.64 ft^2) should provide little resistance to airflow at this size for either case.

Close the chart and loop dialog box and edit path number 3 by double clicking on it. Set the Orifice Area to 10 m^2, set it as Sized and click the OK button. Open the Loop 2 properties again and see the minimum size for Aorfc2 (path 2) is given as 1.023 m^2. Set the orifice area of the UpperWindow (path 2) to 1.023 m^2 (11.01 ft^2) and set its Sized property. Repeat this process to set the orifice area of Clerestory (path 1) to 1.71 m^2 (18.41 ft^2). Now that all of the openings have been sized, when you display the loop properties, the Total Pressure Drop (RHS) value for the case you are sizing (Wind & Stack) should be very close to zero.

You can now analyze this design by running the simulation vie the **Calculations -> Run Simulation** menu command. This will perform a steady state airflow calculation using the CONTAM simulation engine. The SketchPad will now be in the Results Display mode as indicated by the scaled lines (red = pressure difference and green = airflow rate) emanating from the flow paths. You can hide the pressure loops and highlight the path icons to view the simulation results and compare them with the design values as shown in the figure below. Note the fractional bias (FB) provides a means to compare the simulation results to the design values.

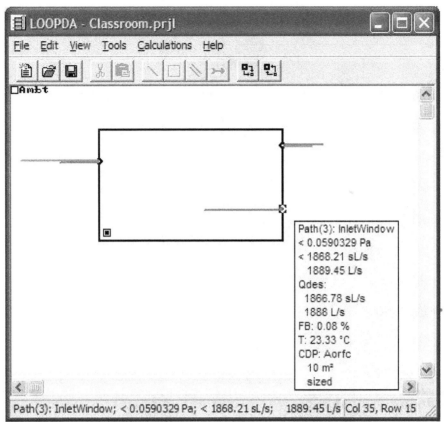

SketchPad display of analysis calculation (ContamX simulation) results

You could then repeat these steps to size the openings for the Stack Only case and other weather conditions. You should save this project file under a new name to work with the next set of condition. You can unsize all the elements via the **Calculations -> Unsize All Elements** command to begin the process.

References

1. Axley, J. W. (2001a). *Residential Passive Ventilation Systems: Evaluation and Design*. AIVC Technical Note 54. International Energy Agency, Coventry.

2. Axley, J.W. (2001b) *Application of Natural Ventilation for U.S. Commercial Buildings*. GCR-01-820 NISTIR 6781, National Institute of Standards and Technology.

3. Emmerich, S.J., W.S. Dols, and J.W. Axley. (2001) *Natural Ventilation Review and Plan for Design and Analysis Tools*. NISTIR 6781, National Institute of Standards and Technology.

4. Dols, W.S., and S.J. Emmerich. (2003) *LoopDA - Natural Ventilation Design and Analysis Software*. NISTIR 6967, National Institute of Standards and Technology.

5. Emmerich, S. J. and W. S. Dols (2003). *LoopDA: A Natural Ventilation System Design and Analysis Tool*. Eight International IBPSA Conference, Eindhoven, Netherlands, IBPSA.

6. Walton, G. N. and W. S. Dols (2005). *CONTAM 2.4 User Guide and Program Documentation*. National Institute of Standards and Technology.

7. ASHRAE. 2009. *Fundamental Handbook*. American Society of Heating, Refrigerating, Air-conditioning Engineers. Atlanta.

8. Irving, S. and E. Uys. *CIBSE Applications Manual: Natural Ventilation in Non-domestic Buildings*. 1997, CIBSE: London.

9. Daly, A. 2003. *LoopDA Testing and Evaluation Report*. Taylor Engineering. Alameda.

Acknowledgements

The authors would like to acknowledge James W. Axley for his work in the area of the design of natural ventilation systems and Alan Daly of Taylor Engineering for his review and comment on LoopDA 1.0 that lead to several of the enhancement made to this version of the tool.